It's Raining Cats and Dogs

by Polly Peterson • illustrated by Tuko Fujisaki

Harcourt

Orlando   Boston   Dallas   Chicago   San Diego

Visit *The Learning Site!*

www.harcourtschool.com

Have you ever heard someone say, "It's raining cats and dogs"? Does this really mean that cats and dogs are falling from the sky?

No, it means that it's raining very hard.
How else can you describe the sound of heavy
rain? Here's another way to say it: "The rain is
coming down in buckets." Can you imagine if
buckets really fell from the sky?

"The rain is coming down in buckets" is a special kind of expression. It is a colorful picture made with words. "It's raining cats and dogs" is another one. Word pictures like these give us new ways to say what we mean.

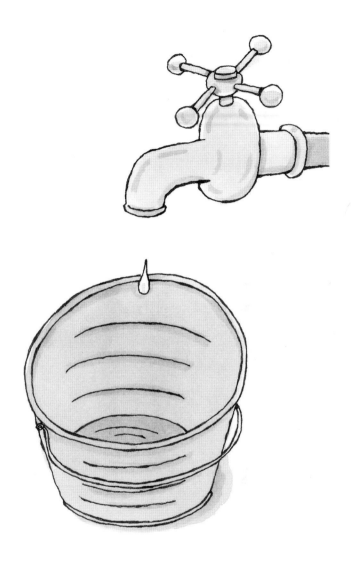

Have you ever heard this expression: "That's just a drop in the bucket?" What do you think it means?

A bucket with just one drop of water in it is almost empty. You need many drops of water to fill a bucket. So you could use this expression, "a drop in the bucket," to describe something that helps a little, but not much.

How do you feel when it's your turn to speak in front of the whole class? Do you feel nervous? Do you get a funny feeling in your stomach?

What's a good way to explain this feeling?
You could use this expression: "I have
butterflies in my stomach." How would it feel
to have a tummy full of butterflies?

Suppose you were worried about a test. What if you were waiting to meet your baby sister for the first time? How could you describe that feeling?

You could use this expression: "I'm on pins and needles." Who could relax on a big pile of pins and needles? Doesn't that word picture describe how you would feel?

Imagine you are looking for something you can't find. You could say this: "I'm looking for a needle in a haystack." Why do people use this expression?

A needle is very small. Can you imagine
how hard it would be to find just one needle in
a big stack of hay? How would you even start
to look?

Has this ever happened to you? You know something, but you can't quite remember it. You could describe this feeling with this expression: "It's right on the tip of my tongue."

If you act very silly, a friend might say you are "going bananas." Another friend might say, "Stop monkeying around." Don't worry. Your friends are just using expressions to describe your actions.

Have you ever heard someone say: "I'm all ears"? It doesn't mean they have giant ears. It just means they are listening very carefully to what is being said.

Do you wish you could remember all the special expressions in this book? Then you should "learn them by heart." That means you will never forget them!